DEC 1 9 2018

W9-AAE-264

Europe

ALICIA KLEPEIS

Rourke
Educational Media

rourkeeducationalmedia.com

Before & After Reading Activities

Before Reading:

Building Academic Vocabulary and Background Knowledge

Before reading a book, it is important to tap into what your child or students already know about the topic. This will help them develop their vocabulary, increase their reading comprehension, and make connections across the curriculum.

1. *Look at the cover of the book. What will this book be about?*
2. *What do you already know about the topic?*
3. *Let's study the Table of Contents. What will you learn about in the book's chapters?*
4. *What would you like to learn about this topic? Do you think you might learn about it from this book? Why or why not?*
5. *Use a reading journal to write about your knowledge of this topic. Record what you already know about the topic and what you hope to learn about the topic.*
6. *Read the book.*
7. *In your reading journal, record what you learned about the topic and your response to the book.*
8. *After reading the book complete the activities below.*

Content Area Vocabulary
Read the list. What do these words mean?

caravans
continent
currency
democracy
ethnic groups
fjords
legumes
maritime
monarchies
service jobs

After Reading:

Comprehension and Extension Activity

After reading the book, work on the following questions with your child or students in order to check their level of reading comprehension and content mastery.

1. What is the landscape like in Europe? (Summarize)
2. What differences might a visitor notice when traveling from one European country to another? (Infer)
3. How have people's lives changed in Europe throughout its history? (Asking questions)
4. Have you seen any European landmarks? If so, which ones? (Text to self connection)
5. What are some reasons that people in Europe might eat different kinds of foods from each other? (Asking questions)

Extension Activity

After reading the book, try this activity. Pick a European country you are interested in and research its capital city. What kinds of places does this city offer for tourists to visit? What languages are spoken there? How does this city compare to where you live? Draw a simple map of the city, labeling any natural features (rivers, mountains, etc.).

Table of Contents

Countries in Europe:

- Albania
- Andorra
- Austria
- Belarus
- Belgium
- Bosnia and Herzegovina
- Bulgaria
- Croatia
- Cyprus
- Czech Republic
- Denmark
- Estonia
- Finland
- France
- Germany
- Greece
- Hungary
- Iceland
- Ireland
- Italy
- Kazakstan
- Kosovo
- Latvia
- Liechtenstein
- Lithuania
- Luxembourg
- Macedonia
- Malta
- Moldova
- Monaco
- Montenegro
- Netherlands
- Norway
- Poland
- Portugal
- Romania
- Russia
- San Marino
- Serbia
- Slovakia
- Slovenia
- Spain
- Sweden
- Switzerland
- Turkey
- Ukraine
- United Kingdom (made up of England, Northern Ireland, Scotland, and Wales)
- Vatican City

Welcome to Europe!

Giant glaciers. Beautiful beaches. Incredible islands. Europe has all these things and more.

Europe is the second smallest **continent** on Earth. Only Australia is smaller. Europe covers an area of 10.18 million square miles (26.37 million square kilometers). It's just a little larger than the United States.

Despite its smaller size, Europe has more people than any continents except Asia and Africa.

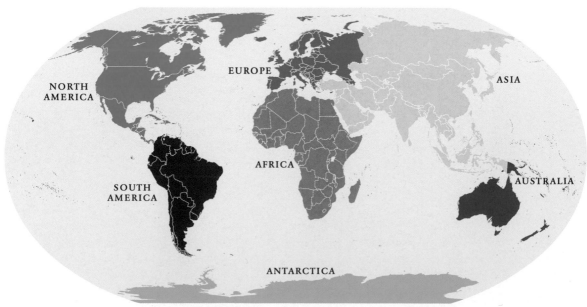

This image of the globe shows all seven continents.

Where is Europe located? All of Europe is in the Northern Hemisphere. Several water bodies border Europe. To the north is the Arctic Ocean. To the west is the Atlantic Ocean. The Mediterranean Sea lies south of Europe.

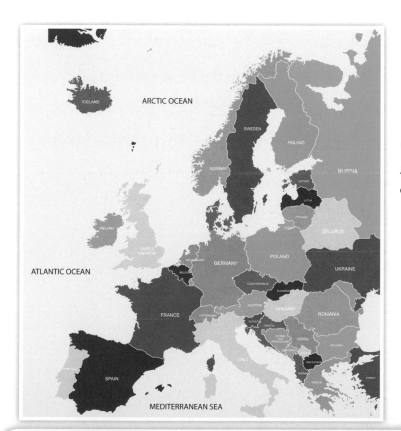

This political map shows all of the countries in Europe.

As one travels farther north in Europe, the weather gets colder. But warm winds from the Atlantic Ocean blow over Europe. These winds make the winters of Norway, Ireland, and the United Kingdom (UK) milder than they would be otherwise. Much of southern Europe has hot, dry summers and rainy, mild winters.

The Ural Mountains serve as a natural border between the continents of Europe and Asia. Other European mountain ranges include the Pyrenees and Caucasus Mountains. Lots of people travel to the Alps to ski in the winter.

More than half of Europe's land is flat, low plains. Many rivers flow through Europe. The Rhine River flows from the Alps to the North Sea. The Volga River winds its way through Russia.

Norway is a narrow but long country in northern Europe. This nation is famous for its beautiful coastline. Norway has **fjords,** which are narrow inlets of the sea located between steep slopes or cliffs. The water of these fjords is often bright blue. Both Norway's fjords and its mountains were carved out by glaciers.

Hebrides Islands, Scotland

Europe has many beautiful and fascinating islands. Visitors from around the world vacation there. Sicily is one example. So are the Dalmatian Islands of Croatia. Tourists also flock to Scotland's Hebrides Islands.

Animal & Plant Life

Europe is home to a variety of plants and animals. Some of these are found nowhere else on Earth.

Parts of northern and northeastern Europe have evergreen forests. Spruce, pine, larch, and fir trees grow here. Some sections of southeastern Europe have grasslands. The Mediterranean region is home to many plants that don't need much water. Cypress and olive trees are two examples.

Both olive trees and grapevines grow in Tuscany, Italy.

People throughout history have chopped down Europe's trees. Why? They wanted to use the land for farming or other purposes. But Europe still has many dense forests. The forestry business remains an important part of Europe's economy to this day.

The Netherlands is known around the globe for its flowers, especially tulips. Some people call this nation the "flower shop of the world." In the spring, visitors to the Netherlands can see huge tulip fields in many bright colors. There are also many tulip festivals around the country every spring.

Some European animals only live in remote areas. The beaver and the red wolf are such creatures. European brown bears live in mountainous areas. They can be found in the Carpathian and Balkan Mountains, for example. These bears snooze the winter away. But other animals live right alongside people. In fact, there are about 33,000 red foxes living in the cities and towns of the UK!

Red foxes were first reported in the 1930s in towns in southern England. These animals have a varied diet, including birds, small mammals, insects, and berries.

Lots of different kinds of birds live in Europe. These include kingfishers, flamingoes, puffins, and nightingales. Some of Europe's birds migrate to Africa when the weather gets cold. There they can find food more easily. One example is the European swallow.

A group of flamingoes wades in the waters of the Ebro River Delta in northeastern Spain.

Not all animals in Europe live on land. There are also many marine creatures here. Seals and more than 45 species of sharks live in the Mediterranean Sea. Europe's lakes, rivers, and seas are home to lots of different fish. Herring, tuna, cod and sardines are just a few.

History & Government

People have lived in Europe for many thousands of years. The first people in Europe were hunters and gatherers. Over time, people learned to farm. They lived in villages where they raised animals and grew crops.

About 4,000 years ago, people in Greece started building cities. They were initially ruled by kings. But about 500 BCE, Athens introduced **democracy**, or government by the people.

Athens, Greece

Maritime trade has been important to Europe throughout its history. This trade brought wealth to many people. It also helped build contacts between the different peoples of Europe. Ideas, foods, and cultures spread throughout the region.

Europe is home to countries large and small. Russia is bigger than the United States. But Europe also has very tiny countries called microstates. Monaco is one example. It takes up less than one square mile (2.59 square kilometers) of land. That's only about three times the size of Washington D.C.'s National Mall! Other microstates in Europe are Vatican City and San Marino.

Monte Carlo, Monaco

The period from about 500 to 1500 CE was known as the Middle Ages. During this time there were many wars. Different groups of people took over various sections of Europe. The Saxons were powerful in England. The Goths took control in Italy and Spain. Christianity became the main religion in Europe during the Middle Ages.

This painting of Saint Martin cutting a piece of his cloak can be viewed in the Saint Gatien's Cathedral in Tours, France. Saint Martin lived during the 4th century CE.

The Renaissance was an important period in European history. It took place from about 1300 to 1600 CE. During this time there were many advancements in art, science, and education. Life improved for many people.

Italian painter Raphael painted The School of Athens *between 1509 and 1511. This Renaissance masterpiece is part of the Vatican Museum's art collection.*

World Wars I and II happened during the 20th century. More than 75 million people were killed worldwide during these wars.

The European Union (EU) was created in 1993. This organization is made up of more than 25 European countries. Their governments work together. The EU makes it easier for people to travel freely within Europe. These countries trade goods and services with each other. They share a common **currency**, the euro.

World War I cemetery in France, Vimy La Targette

Not every country in Europe has the same type of government. Several countries are **monarchies**. Examples include Belgium and the United Kingdom. The kings and queens usually do not run the government. Most European nations have a republican form of government. This means the people hold supreme power. They elect officials who represent their interests in the government.

Born in 1926, Queen Elizabeth II has served as monarch of the United Kingdom since 1953. She is the longest reigning monarch in British history.

The People of Europe

About 743 million people live in Europe. Europeans belong to a variety of **ethnic groups**. These groups often have their own traditions, celebrations, and ways of life. An example is the Roma people. They live in many European nations. They speak a language called Romani and often travel together in **caravans**.

A Roma family poses in front of their caravan. It is believed that the Roma originally came from India.

Europeans speak many different languages. The Romance languages include Italian, Spanish and French. Germanic languages include English, German and the Scandinavian languages. Russian, Czech and Polish are all Slavic languages.

Languages in Europe

Germanic languages
English
German
Swedish
Danish
Norwegian
Dutch
Frisian
Icelandic
Faroese
Luxembourgish

Slavic languages
Russian
Polish
Ukrainian
Czech
Belarusian
Slovak
Serbo Croatian
Slovenian
Bulgarian
Macedonian
Sorbian

Romance languages
French
Italian
Spanish
Portuguese
Catalan
Galician
Romansh
Furlan
Ladin
Corsican
Sardinian
Aromanian
Romanian

Uralic languages
Hungarian
Finnish
Estonian
Sami
Karelian
Komi
other Uralic languages

Celtic languages
Welsh
Irish
Scottish Gaelic
Breton
Manx

Altaic languages
Turkish
Azeri
Kalmyk
Gagauz
Bashkir
other Altaic languages

Baltic languages
Lithuanian
Latvian

Basque
Maltese
Albanian
Greek

Kurdish
Georgian
Armenian
Ossetian

Abkhazian

other Caucasian languages

Scale
1 / 6.000.000

The Sami people live in Norway, Sweden, Finland, and Russia. They have their own unique culture. Traditionally, the Sami followed the migrating reindeer herds of the Arctic. The Sami used all parts of the reindeer to meet their needs. They made tents and clothing from hides. They even made twine from the animals' tendons!

Christianity is the main religion in nearly every country in Europe. Christians across the continent celebrate some of the same holidays. Easter and Christmas are two examples. Jewish people live throughout Europe. Muslims also live in countries all over Europe. They make up the majority of people in Turkey, Albania, Bosnia, and Herzegovina.

A Christmas tree stands in front of Saint Vitus Cathedral in Prague, Czech Republic. This cathedral was built over nearly 600 years.

People in Europe do all kinds of work. About 70 percent of Europeans work in **service jobs**. They might have jobs at banks or shops. Or they could work in hospitals or schools. Some Europeans work on farms. Others work in mines or factories.

Some of the world's coolest cars come from Europe. You may have seen a favorite celebrity roll up to an event in a flashy Ferrari or Lamborghini. Both of these car manufacturers are in Italy. BMW and Mercedes-Benz are German car companies. And the 2017 (German) Volkswagen e-Golf car gets 119 miles (191.5 kilometers) per gallon of gas!

Food & Fun

Just like people all over the world, Europeans love to eat and have fun. They also create amazing art, music, and literature.

Europe has produced many talented artists. Vincent van Gogh (1853 - 1890) was a Dutch painter. He created works such as *The Starry Night*. Italian artist Michelangelo (1475 - 1564) is known for his realistic sculptures of people. His painting of the Sistine Chapel attracts visitors from all over the globe. And modern-day artist Christo creates outdoor artworks. He once wrapped Paris's Point Neuf Bridge in fabric!

Vincent van Gogh painted The Starry Night *in 1889 while in France. Today this painting is on display at the Museum of Modern Art in New York.*

People enjoy a variety of sports in Europe. Soccer is the most popular. Cricket, a game played with a bat and wickets, is also well-liked in many European countries. Throughout Europe, people hike as an outdoor activity. Switzerland has thousands of miles of well-marked hiking trails. These are popular with both locals and visitors.

Every winter the city of Venice, Italy, holds an annual festival called Carnival. This Christian festival ends forty days before Easter at the start of Lent. The festival is famous for the elaborate masks and costumes people wear. As many as a million visitors come to Venice each year to take part in this special festival.

Activity: Play Boules

Boules is an outdoor ball game played in Europe. It is especially popular in France. Traditionally, people play using special metallic balls on a flat-but-level dirt surface. Here are the basics for how to play:

Supplies:

- 6 balls of the same size, about 3 inches (8 centimeters) in diameter (these are your boules)
- 1 smaller ball, about 1.25 inches (3 centimeters) in diameter (this is your jack)
- A flat surface
- A stick or chalk
- A coin
- Measuring tape

Directions (For Two Players):

1. Each player gets three boules. The jack is shared.

2. Draw a circle on the ground. It should be about 18 inches (46 centimeters) in diameter. Players must stand in this circle when playing. Both of their feet have to stay on the ground.

3. Toss a coin to see which player gets to place the jack. Each player must call heads or tails.

4. Whoever wins the coin toss gets to throw the jack. It can be tossed in any direction but should land about 13 to 26 feet (4 to 8 meters) away from the circle. The jack should be at least 3 feet (1 meter) from any object.

5. Once the jack is in place, the first player stands in the circle and tosses one boule aiming to get the boule as close to the jack as possible. It's acceptable to knock the other player's boule farther away from the jack.

6. The second player stands in the circle and tosses one boule, trying to get the boule even closer to the jack than the first player. Each player alternates tossing their boules until they have tossed all three. One point goes to the player who gets the ball closes

7. Start a new round by drawing a circle around the jack. Toss the jack again and repeat tossing the boules, three per round, until one player reaches 13 points.

Many Europeans travel to seaside resorts for vacation. Tallinn in Estonia is a popular destination. So is Bodrum in Turkey. Here people can try sports from scuba diving to boating. Or they can just sunbathe on a beach, of course!

Food is also an important part of European culture. Different countries often have their own special dishes. Some regions share common ingredients or spices. For example, the Mediterranean diet often includes olive oil, fresh fruits and vegetables, **legumes**, whole grains, and fish.

Bodrum, Turkey

Recipe–Ratatouille

Ratatouille is a popular dish in many European countries. You will need an adult helper to make this meal.

Ingredients
- 1 large eggplant
- 2 bell peppers (green or any color work well)
- 3 tomatoes
- 1 big zucchini
- 1 large or 2 small onions
- 3 cloves garlic, minced
- $\frac{1}{4}$ cup (59 mL) olive oil
- $\frac{1}{2}$-$\frac{3}{4}$ cup (118-177 mL) cold water
- $\frac{1}{2}$ teaspoon (2.5 mL) dried basil
- salt and pepper (to taste)
- vegetable bouillon (to taste)

Directions: Peel eggplant, zucchini, onion, and garlic. Wash all the other vegetables. Have an adult help you cut all vegetables into chunks about $\frac{1}{2}$ inch (1.27 cm) in size. Place all of the veggies and garlic into a large saucepan. Mix in the oil, pepper, basil and cold water. Bring to a boil, then turn down and let simmer in a covered pan for about an hour until all vegetables are soft. Once it boils, add a cube or two of vegetable bouillon for flavor. Mash with a potato masher or pestle.

It is common to serve this dish over couscous but you can also use rice. Or just enjoy it like a soup with a spoon!

Landmarks

Some of the world's most famous landmarks are located in Europe. Here are just a few of these beautiful buildings and clever creations!

St. Basil's Cathedral is in Moscow, Russia. This church was constructed between 1555 and 1561. It is known for its brightly colored onion domes. But it was not so colorful when it was first built.

Ever dream of living in a castle? King Ludwig II of Germany was lucky enough to call Neuschwanstein Castle home. Tucked into the Bavarian Alps, this castle has fairytale views.

One of the most famous European landmarks is the Parthenon. It's located in Athens, Greece. This temple was dedicated to the goddess of wisdom, Athena. It was built of white marble in the 5th century BCE. Its huge columns and beautiful remaining sculptures still impress visitors.

In the Swedish village of Jukkasjärvi is an unusual modern landmark: the Icehotel. It lies 200 miles north of the Arctic Circle. This hotel made of ice and snow was first built in 1989. New artists build the rooms out of ice each year.

It may seem strange but one amazing European landmark lies underground. The Channel Tunnel, aka the Chunnel, connects France and England by rail. Construction began in 1988 and ended in 1993. Passenger train service began in 1994. More than 23 miles (37 kilometers) of the Chunnel lies under the English Channel. It is the longest undersea tunnel on Earth!

Glossary

caravans (KAR-uh-vanz): covered vehicles, particularly those equipped to live in while traveling

continent (KANT-uhn-ent): one of the world's great divisions of land, such as Europe, Asia, or North America

currency (KUHR-uhn-see): a system of money used in a particular country

democracy (di-MOWK-ruh-see): a government in which the people choose their leaders

ethnic groups (ETH-nik GRUPZ): populations or communities of people who share a common cultural tradition or descent

fjords (fee-ORDZ): narrow inlets of the sea located between steep slopes or cliffs

legumes (leg-YOOMZ): the parts (such as seeds or pods) of certain leguminous plants used as food; legumes include beans and peas

maritime (MAR-uh-time): of or relating to trade or navigation on the sea

monarchies (MAHN-uhr-keez): countries or nations ruled by monarchs (especially kings, queens, or emperors)

service jobs (SUHR-viss JOBZ): jobs in which a worker provides some type of useful labor but does not produce goods

Index

Show What You Know

1. Where is Europe located?
2. What are some popular vacation spots in Europe?
3. How does Europe compare in size to the other continents?
4. What is the weather like in Europe?
5. What kinds of jobs do people have in Europe?

Further Reading

Baxter, Roberta, *Learning About Europe*, Lerner, 2016.

Hirsch, Rebecca, *Europe*, Scholastic, 2013.

Aertker, Paul, *Crime Travelers*, Flying Solo Press LLC, 2014.

About the Author

From vampires to jellybeans, Alicia Klepeis loves to research fun and out-of-the-ordinary topics that bring the world to young readers. Alicia began her career at the National Geographic Society. A former middle school teacher, she is the author of more than seventy children's books including *A Time for Change, Trolls*, and *Haunted Cemeteries Around The World*. Alicia has lived in both France and England but hopes to explore more of Europe in the future. She lives with her family in upstate New York.

Meet The Author!
www.meetREMauthors.com

© 2019 Rourke Educational Media

All rights reserved. No part of this book may be reproduced or utilized in any form or by any means, electronic or mechanical including photocopying, recording, or by any information storage and retrieval system without permission in writing from the publisher.

www.rourkeeducationalmedia.com

PHOTO CREDITS: Cover: ©yulenochekk, ©RomanBabakin, ©IakovKalinin, ©George Clerk; page header: ©fergregory; p. 6: ©CasarsaGuru; p. 7: ©Nataliya Hora; p. 8: ©FCerez; p. 9: ©abadonian; p. 10: ©skibreck; p. 11: ©mafrmcfa; p. 12: ©Klaus Hollitzer; p. 14: ©Jorisvo; p. 15: ©Wiki; p. 16: ©Willequet Manuel; p. 17: ©UK MoD Crown; p. 18: ©Barry Lewis/©Alamy Stock Photo; p. 19: ©Wiki; p. 20: ©Borut Trdina;p. 21: ©monkeybusinessimages; p. 22: ©Wiki; p. 23: ©ablokhin; p. 24: ©Michael Löffler; p. 26: ©slava296; p. 27: ©OlgaLepeshkina; p. 29: ©Dan77.

Edited by: Keli Sipperley
Cover and Interior design by: Rhea Magaro-Wallace

Library of Congress PCN Data

Europe / Alicia Klepeis
(Earth's Continents)
ISBN 978-1-64156-411-3 (hard cover)
ISBN 978-1-64156-537-0 (soft cover)
ISBN 978-1-64156-661-2 (e-Book)
Library of Congress Control Number: 2018930432

Rourke Educational Media
Printed in the United States of America,
North Mankato, Minnesota